QUENTIN S. CRISP
SEPTEMBER

Memories no one
Ever will track to events:
How old was I, at
Whose home, on what occasion?
They have flown history's law.

I could not have watched,
At the London flat of a
Friend of my father,
The Planet of the Spiders,
T.V. bright, night dark outside.

The caravan park
Where my mother cleaned could not
Have been so close to
Sand dunes on a misty day.
A door left open. Escape.

Shirts and T-shirt hang
From the curtain rod. I fear
This morning what the
Day will commandeer me for.
Car noises soft and nervous.

Wednesday, 2nd

Waking very late
I suddenly remember
In pins-and-needles
Who I am: this here, this now.
Can this transparency die?

Distance. Is distance
The important thing, seeing
The world through writing?
But perhaps nothing has more
Distance than simply living.

I've felt the strangeness
Of my life before, as if
I cannot die, when
I jarred my head in a bed
In Wales, long-term unemployed.

Again this morning,
Sun, on the smooth fake-hardwood
Floor. It quivers there
Like wind chimes without wind or
Sound. A golden blush, then gone.

I walk out the door
At the turn of the season
And anticipate,
Subtler than any incense,
A caress, of damp, of chill.

Now I'm forty-three
I anticipate and find
I'm validated.
But what is this scent as blue
As the sky, brown as dead leaves?

It's almost like I
Read that scent the way I read
Sophisticated
Velvety autumnal tales
By Tanizaki or Gide.

Last night was the first
Distinct occasion this year.
Passing the front yards
Of others' houses, I grew
Warm, shivered with the soft thrill.

Thursday, 3rd

Aurelius writes:
"To love only what happens".
I hear the drip, drip
Of the immersion heater.
Anyway, I can love this.

What are the floor tiles
(Fake) in my bathroom made of?
After my shower,
Shaving, my feet bare, they feel
Like a freshly used wetsuit.

Heavy metal night
At the King's Arms. Talk of an
Economist who
Warned a new crisis draws near
And said we must print money.

Hallways—I love them.
In mine, junk mail piles up and
Jackets hang from hooks.
A wardrobe, broom-cupboard-like,
Begins to smell of autumn.

Yesterday I took
A mildewed, black suit-jacket
Into town, to find
A good dry cleaner's. I wish
Life was made of such errands.

The end of the world
Implies that all we know and
Wider is to go.
Sighing in that 'wider', I
Think, "Let's just enjoy it, then."

Saturday, 5th

Walking through Acton
Estate, the densely packed heart
Of London. Concrete
Tessellation. From unseen
Lives, wafts of marijuana.

All dry cleaners have
One thing in common. You step
On the mat inside
The door and set off a chime.
Who decreed it would be so?

Morning. A flurry
Of travel cards and tickets.
From the top deck of
A bus, between brick buildings,
A weedy glimpse of canal.

George asks if I know
The English word—not the French—
For 'horizon', as
'Bill of fare' is to 'menu'.
Maybe. But no. It's 'skysill'.

Mapledurham Lock.
A place is also a time.
I could recommend
That you visit the river,
But the place has gone downstream.

On a rotten stump
At the river's edge, 'a perch'.
This could be the noun
For a group of herons if
Each was not so singular.

Sunday, 6th

In the dream I crashed
George's boat into a tree.
Branches swept stove pipes
Into the river. I woke
And remembered it was true.

In the dream there was
A girl. We were splitting up.
"You have no sense of
Purpose," I said. She said, "But
I have feelings." Dear girl.

Culham Lock was slow
To fill. I looked for a place
To piss. A concrete
Chicane-screen; where does this go?
An old, roofless urinal.

Unbelievable,
The houses whose gardens slope
To the river bank.
Among water-dipping trees
We twice glimpsed kingfisher blue.

Second-hand market.
Greenwich. On one table a
Potpourri of old
Costume jewellery. Even
I think it's worthless. How sad.

Sun slants through oak leaves
In the rolling park. We came
Here a year ago.
There are more deer now in the
Hide. As day declines I'm glad.

From transport routes you
Might get the impression that
Greenwich and Blackheath
Are not pressed cheek to cheek. We
Step from one into the next.

It's getting dark. In
Search of fish and chips we find
A French bistro with
Blankets on some chairs outside.
Next to us, two first-daters.

Tuesday, 8th

The aggression of
All these threats of damnation.
"You will die and I
Won't." Conflation of winning
With virtue, sometimes subtle.

So far: the present
Plus memory can be an
Unsatisfying
Edge. But sometimes autumn's like
The crust on an old carpet.

The morning duvet
When I've just got up is like
Fallen leaves, strangely
Cool, mellowly unclean, a
Vacant slackness; free, flat bliss.

I have deadlines, bills,
Obligations. Why does this
Feel so much like the
End of the world? Why does this
Feel so much like damnation?

The difficulty
Of modern life is that the
Claims others make on
Your indebtedness are so
Various and conflicting.

Night. Antiphony
On a bus from Abingdon
To Oxford: "What do
You think of Swindon?" "Shit!" "What
Do you think of shit?" "Swindon!"

Wednesday, 9th

On Sunday it seemed
There might be a reprise of
Summer. With each day
That slips by, the chances of
That grow slimmer, skies dimmer.

When does autumn start?
I'll have to look it up. I
Love September as
An ecotone, between two
Domains, like a riverbank.

The cool of autumn,
Or late summer, is not yet
The chill of winter.
I can wear pyjamas, still,
Around the flat. It soothes me.

Ornaments in Jade
Lies atop my bookcase. A
Slim volume, hardback,
Recently read. And so? Of
Such mellow sadness, is home.

Bikini wax ads
Remind me that the human
Race perpetuates
Itself through prods, nods and lures,
Through gameshow vulgarity.

It's eerie to think
That in dreams, when I feel least
Alone, I am most.
Awake, I can't imagine;
Asleep, I invent like God.

A carver's at work
In Bursted Wood. From broken
Trees appear whittled
Birds, a frog, a rat; someone
Stole an owl, predictably.

Tom G. Warrior's
Latest band, Triptykon, is
A ribbed, black, writhing
Serpent of anti-life, a
Photo-negative of joy.

The gentleness of
Autumn, the fertility
Of later things—I
Would convey this. Soft as leaf
Litter; brilliant as leaves.

Where Celtic Frost stood
Thirty years ago, I stand
Now, largely unknown,
Limited editions bought
And read by a morbid few.

Friday, 11th

Things that were new grow
Old. 'Loving the Alien'
Is not the same song
Today as it was even
In two thousand and seven.

As if the cosmos
Would falter if I didn't
Develop my notes
Into a novel! But I
Am all that's still to play for.

Iterations of
The cosmic: Lovecraft with his
Slimy octopi;
Lu Yun, the Chinese poet,
With seasons in his cottage.

'Komorebi', a
Poetic Japanese noun
That means sunlight through
Branches. I need a word that
Adds to this, 'through net curtains'.

"But what if you're wrong?"
"About my existence?" Times
I've asked myself this
Question, my whole being asks
And replies, a somersault.

Signs that I'm alive:
Saturday breezes from a
Window. Upstairs, known
Voices talking. My faith is
Just this, now and forever.

I will give myself
Wholly to breakfast. How else
To overcome the
Weight of eternity, of
Death, and of my welling guilt?

Clouds cover the sun.
The shadows of net curtains
Appear, revolve
And disappear. Doubt and
Faith revolve in me like this.

Saturday, 12th

There is poetry
In life. On Regent's Canal
I bought a book of
Chinese philosophy. Tired,
Later, nodded off reading.

Can a mind be like
Dead wood, ashes? asked Tzŭ-yu.
Yes. Looking from a
Kitchen window at London's
Garden sheds, an apple tree.

Sometimes I feel such
Sadness that even if the
Universe divulged
To me its personal love,
I'd huff like a jobless ghost.

For some, a monster;
For others, shelter. Buddha
Sat beneath one. Christ
Was nailed upon one. Sinews
Joining earth and sky, a tree.

Many-limbed gallows.
How often has this been the
Revolving mobile
Of history? How often
The greenwood tree of outlaws?

Life and death. Tree and
Serpent. How Triptykon stores
Energy using
Inversion. Even now there
Is growth; branches stir anew.

One saying runs through
Latin, English, Mandarin:
Man proposes; God
Disposes. It is chaos,
In the end, that will save us.

The ninth of August.
Rise, ghosts of earth. Bursted Wood
Glimmered with web, in
The sinking sun. I catch sight
Of an antlered god, enthroned.

Monday, 14th

Marcus. I wonder
Why he didn't keep in touch.
His life now is too
Different, perhaps. Is mine?
Are those furtive days all done?

He made me mix-tapes.
I recall, on one of these,
I first heard David
Sylvian. "The ghosts of my
Life blow wilder than before."

I simply cannot
Get everything done. What's left
When you realise
This? Death-bed memories. They
Are accounted differently.

That pale skin. You think
Those provincial days were a
Nullity. What you
Didn't know what to do with
Will most ravish you at last.

Occasionally my
Hibiscus will spread out a
Flower. She seems to
Do this overnight. I guess
If I rose early, I'd see.

In the petals, veins make
Beauty, like a butterfly's
Wing. Fragility
Of living things. Why don't we
See the life in human veins?

My bitterness at
The toxin of the doxa.
The geeks inherit
The Earth—see how they use it.
Anti-human humanists.

There is a leaning
Sundial in a grassy
Garden, a brick from
A nearby pile in place of
Its gnomon. Sehnsucht o'clock.

Monday, 14th

Tuesday, 15th

Realisation
Of death comes in waves. The same
Realisation
Feels new, seems different. I wish
The waves would empty and stop.

The only thing to
Deal with is now, various
Wise people state, to
Reassure us. Yes, but now
Moves. What moves might also crash.

So die now, runs the
Advice, and everything will
Be the afterlife.
But dying is no act of
Will. No, I wait to be killed.

The ultimate truth
Being death—life thus without
Meaning—why balk at
Dying? You sense something in
Life, by death not overcome.

Not overcome by
Death, why balk at dying? There
Lies the knot of faith.
Nihilists, to cut that knot,
Determined, equivocate.

'To hang up the phone'.
The verb's half-archaic now.
As a writer I
Eschew time-bound words, though such
Untranslatables spell life.

When I grow weary,
Or sick with dismay at my
Aging towards death,
I remember that pristine
Creative process called 'dream'.

Evenings are colder.
Mornings, too. I wear a brown,
Knitted shawl. I have
Two mothers. This shawl, one gave
To the other, she to me.

I only want peace
Now. Peace excites me enough.
Van Gogh's *Sunflowers*
Over the latest SF
Blockbuster. In art; in life.

Thursday, 17th

I suppose I feel
This is the September of
My life. Some might say,
With lifespans stretching, it's more
Like my August. Well, who cares?

I used to think that
Literature belonged to youth,
As beauty does. What
Untold agony for youth
To pass in obscurity!

Literature's function
Is twofold. First, to keep from
Dying. Second, to
Learn to die. Whatever I
Write, I won't keep from dying.

Then let me read of
Talking animals who live
Beneath the earth—mice,
Weasels, badgers, shrews—with the
One I love, the one I love.

Des Esseintes I am
Not, but I know how to frame
A day with tea-lights,
Chakôro, and the scent of
Roasting tea: my engine room.

"Sick on a journey."
So ended Bashô's life. Times
I feel sick, I wish
That I could sleep, on a boat,
When it's raining, out to sea.

Lewis cites *The Well
At the World's End* for its ring
Of sehnsucht. For me,
'After Dark in the Playing
Fields'. Sweeter than a love song.

Friday, 18th

My neighbour's head swims
By outside my window in
Silence. The routines
Of the building reassure
Me. Why don't my own routines?

Arthur Russell. His
Music reverberates with
The skeletal warmth
Of leafless trees. But I play
It for mood, not for meaning.

Last night, on the patch
Of park by Bursted Wood, I
Felt those breezes that
Greet you from the stillness of
Dark, as intimate as secrets.

Despite frustrations
Of the work variety,
I've been mellow these
Last few days. Thanks to autumn—
That timeless not-mattering?

Red and white floor tiles.
Red and white checked table sheets.
Founding-year photo.
The smell of vinegar, I
Take out into the drizzle.

Ghosts are made by sin.
The greatest sin is that of
Reductionism.
Say that life does not exist
And it comes back as a ghost.

Scientists, these days,
Call it "spooky stuff". What is
It? What Duns Scotus
Calls 'thisness', perhaps? That is,
Whatever's not merely type.

"I'm sorry to have
To tell you this, my friend." This
Is the style they use
For bullying. In whose name?
In the name of 'the people'?

"Because science." So
The argument itself is
Reduced. To slogan,
To *non sequitur*. A bluff
Of how-dare-you. Zombies rule.

Unconscious bias
Is more exasperating
Than the conscious type.
"It's all meaningless," you say.
So why should I talk to you?

Saturday, 19th

Blue-black lipstick. "You
Know that chav? He's actually
Quite nice. He came back
To my flat. No, nothing like
That. He was with his girlfriend."

Three foxes slope from
The roof of one garden shed
To another. They
Live from meal to meal. So why
Are they so restful to watch?

Summer and autumn
Meet in a crucible of
Tender alchemy.
Summer returns and recedes,
Mixing with autumn, makes gold.

There are no brakes. You
Must leap from the door of a
Moving car. Papers
From the back seat float in space
Where the car veered, disappeared.

The thought of death grows
Sweet again, as the thought of
The weekend is to
A temping office worker
On a midweek afternoon.

Monday, 21st

Near Bursted Wood, crows
Caw, that old, acred rattle.
"It's reptilian,"
I say. You point to a tree's
Grey-ridged bark: "It sounds like this."

Even to sehnsucht
There are components. We talked
In an absinthe glow.
Dan struck upon "innocence";
It fitted as key to lock.

Education. We,
Mushroomed, lie beneath a tree.
Kenny Everett,
I recall, looked on such clouds
And said, "Isn't God clever?"

Dao De Jing, verse twelve:
Colours blind you; sounds deafen.
Howard Jones, 'New Song':
Don't be fooled by what you see;
Don't be fooled by what you hear.

The way my mind works—
An insight: in Bursted Wood
The carvings are named.
I called the crow, "Hooded Claw".
We checked and it was Dark Wings.

The crow's rugose voice,
Dry as time, brings to my mind
Ruined castles. Old
Battles turn to peace within
Nature. Crows scatter, wheel, caw.

Amphibians—a
Very special link in life's
Chain. Water dragons.
To be of two worlds. To guard
An old well moist with secrets.

Tuesday, 22nd

The Economist
Is baffled by Mexico's
Lack of free market
Values. They should want exams
And expanded enterprise.

As each new wonder
Is unveiled, those around me
Squeal in amazement.
Last night I grew afraid they
Will find a cure for blindness.

I don't want to live
In the future. I'd prefer
A present where change
Is not *a priori* good
And choices can still be made.

Why are we at peace
In nature? Because there is
A balance between
Chaos and order. The leaves
Repeat asymmetrically.

Rain gently explodes
Any airtight rhythm. So
When it spots and taps
My windows, I feel life breathe—
A shiver that brings me warmth.

Unable to live
In the contradictions of
The Ligottian
View, I found, tentatively,
Reason. Can I turn back now?

News of an old friend.
I'm told he asked after me.
No funding at home,
He's travelling the world. I
Wonder when we'll meet again.

I wanted to write
About parcels in the post
Spotted with rain as
With soft thrills. About death and
This strange yes that it must mean.

Draining the dregs of
The *genmaicha* from my old
Dobin, leaves of sun
Trembling outside and in, could
This slow pace of mine be right?

Wednesday, 23rd

That my roots are in
The wrong soil is implied, or
Said outright sometimes.
What do I do with this thought?
Don't seek reassurance yet.

Or, if you want it,
Here it is: I did not make
The soil from which I
Sprang. Wrong or not, I exist.
Let right, then, do what it must.

T.V. ads give us
Depthless bright visions of all
Phases of human
Life. But they miss out death. Why?
Death included, we'd be safe.

Leyton. Small front yards.
Packed earth scoured over with weeds.
Broken chairs and tiles.
Street overflows for neglect.
There, a cycad dwarfs its house.

Pavements after rain.
Where leaves have fallen, stuck and
Slipped again, they make
Shadows, experiments in
Photography, fresh fossils.

The net curtains here
Are tattered, as from scissors—
Straight. And stained, no doubt
From tobacco smoke. CDs,
Books, DVDs—a haven.

Friday, 25th

Forty-three. On the
Slade Green train, I dig this book
On Voegelin. Back home
I put on Triptykon. As
Byrne said, "How did I get here?"

If Tolstoy, say, were
Time-slipped to the present day,
What frame of reference
Could he use to pass judgement
On our progress or decline?

Was he another
Who renounced literature, like
Gogol, Origen,
Et cetera? You can't be an
Unconscious teacher, he said.

But my lineage
Is exactly that: the school
Of dream. My father,
Jung before him, before him,
Mythology. All exiles.

The draft from under
The spare-room door brings within
Reach those younger days
Of uncertainty like the
Morning start of a journey.

The heaped hours, years, like
Rubbish dumps of questioning,
Migraines of angst, then,
At times, sweetly, flatly, death
Is the easiest nothing.

The greats have struggled
With death and found death greater
(We hear). But it's not
Their business now. Only me
Dealing with me and nothing.

Sunday, 27th

The sinus-stripping
Smell of nail polish returns
To me from distant
Days a tremulous sense of
Experiment, of trying.

Strange and in between,
Memories stir up a sense
Of incompleteness
Like a 'To Be Continued'
That never is; like mildew.

Tea garden. What looks
Like an ivied wall is a
Trellis. Birds—sparrows
And finches—trapeze through leaves,
Squeeze through a chair-back's green mesh.

Gnats in groups of five,
Spinning. I wonder whether
This contains all the
Data to remake the world
After the next big die-off.

Watching them, I try
To trace a single flight and
Think I glimpse beneath
Why Aquinas concluded
There must be a prime mover.

Two and a half years
Have passed. Dominika says
It doesn't seem real
That I'm here. After some thought
I agree. But I am real.

Monday, 28th

You can't see any
Scars, so you will not believe
That the joy in me
Was murdered when I was small.
What's mute is invisible.

The pheasants that die
On the road, I wish someone
Would eat them. No one
Stops for them. Corpses that add
To a value of zero.

Ligotti makes the
Canon. Fame appears designed
To force us to want
Nothing. If so, I don't want
Fame. I don't want nothing, though.

We have time to stop
At the cemetery before
Our lift back. We sit.
Audible now, non-human
Song. A cat watches us go.

Or sometimes I do
Want nothing. Time was, common
Folk could hate the stars.
Now everyone scrabbles for
Pettier fame on Facebook.

Of Taurus: "There are
Some things you just can't do." I
Think of this after
Reading Aurelius. I'm
Number Four, the wicked heart.

So when I despair,
I'm bowing to appearance,
That is, to time. How
Compelling it is! I'm told
That no time passes for light.

Garden spider, with
A cross on your back: you drop
Into place on your
Web, singly from the matrix
Of your eternal species.

Tuesday, 29th

You're right; I have a
Taste for smoky things. You list
Them. Lapsang souchong,
My tea burner, and now these:
Irish smoked oatcakes. What next?

Pop culture's a con.
See how the press colluded
With Morrissey, billed
As 'intelligent' what was
Just 'intelligent-flavoured'.

Mild days after all,
This September. Last night I
Saw a mosaic
Of leaves in mud around a
Tree. The real cold is coming.

Think of the routine
Of getting up each morning
To run a bookshop
In Ilfracombe. What dreams would
Be yours each day? What nightmares?

I think of your coat
On a hook in my sister's
Hallway. Hallways—I
Love them. In between, but
Safe. Your coat will be returned.

It strikes me this word,
'Metaxy', I've encountered,
Is like 'ecotone'.
It gives me hope, focusing
My sense of a writer's role.

Wednesday, 30th

Shivelight. I want to
Use this word, but I'm afraid
It will always be
An allusion to Hopkins.
But he'd want me to use it.

Shivelight. The power
Of evocation in words.
Not only do I
See shafts of light between trees,
I see an ungulate toe.

There are so many
Things I want to do with you.
Buy a takeaway
From the Fortune Star on the
Erith Road. So many things.

www.ingramcontent.com/pod-product-compliance
Lightning Source LLC
Chambersburg PA
CBHW021453080526
44588CB00009B/834